Embrace Yourself

G B BERNHARDS

WORKBOOK PRESS LLC
187 E Warm Springs Rd,
Suite B285, Las Vegas, NV 89119, USA

Website: https://workbookpress.com/
Hotline: 1-888-818-4856
Email: admin@workbookpress.com

Ordering Information:
Quantity sales. Special discounts are available on quantity purchases by corporations, associations, and others.
For details, contact the publisher at the address above.

Library of Congress Control Number:

ISBN-13:   978-1-960752-88-8 (Paperback Version)
                978-1-960752-89-5 (Digital Version)

REV. DATE: 09/21/2022

EMBRACE YOURSELF

BY

G.B. BERNHARDS

INDEX

PAGE

WITHOUT A NAME.

I want to sing

my life away

make you stay.

I want to feel

my soul fly

you wonder why.

I want to love,

You again

Without an end.

I want to know

if reality is sane

or in vain.

My life was

in a dream

didn't see no aim

waited for the time.

I DO TOO

Young boy, you are growing
Young boy, you are changing
Into a man.

Your brown eyes, curly hair
Makes me want to be there
You are changing into a man
Hope life will be fair.

I see you walking on the street
You're a guy I like to meet
Your heart is pounding
You're surrounded with friends and love.

She came from nowhere
Stood on the track
She was someone
To hunt you at last.

You gazed into her blue eyes'
Wanting to touch her hair
She looked cool to me
You liked her more.

You fear not to be able to
You fear not to have her to yourself.

SO DIFFICULT TO FIND.

You say I'm pretty

But you don't hold my hand

You say you love me

But you don't know why

You say it's right

But you know it's wrong

You say it's interesting

But you don't want to change.

Why did you have to be, so special

Why did you have to be, so kind

Why did you have to be, so gentle

Why did you have to be, so blind

Why did you have to be, so difficult to find.

LITTLE CREATURE DON'T CRY.

You are shy in your way
You move I hear myself say
What a face, what a grace,
To have you around.

Through your eyes may not realize
What I feel inside
And my words never give you a clue
I feel my love for you hide in me.

I never touched you like I wanted to
I never said the things I needed to
But when I get home, I sit down,
And dream of you,
I watch myself go deeper into loneliness.

You are a boy to me
You are unspoiled and free
You are like a little animal
Crying in the wind.

If you would change
I love you now as I would then
I love you for who you are
Who are you
I like to know you more.

SWEET TALK.

Don't you leave me

Don't you leave me alone

Don't you tell me

Don't you tell me that I'm crazy

For I already know

That I'm a sweet-talking

Love making lady, yes I am

A sweet-talking

Love making lady

I want to tell you

Anything you want to hear.

Come on closer to me

Don't be chicken

It's only me

I'm a sweet-talking

Love making lady, yes I am.

THE CHALLENGE.

Laying in bed
Thinking how sad
To have lost you this way
Nobody's fault but mine
Wish I wouldn't die but wise enough
To let it slip away
Too late to do anything now.

Wish I were a star
So you would be proud of me
Wish I had a plan
How to get over you
Wish I had what I wanted.

Seeking for something
That I could not find.
Living through this life
Just to waist time
Not wise enough to go away.

We are not the deciders of
When or where
We are to disappear
Life is a challenge to me
I win until
I no longer can.

TO KNOW LOVE.

I know she knows,
That I'm still in love,
I can tell by the way
She looks at me.
He knows he brings out
The best in me.
I feel proud feeling this way.

God knows that, loving him strong,
Will keep me going on.
She knows, I feel like a flame
Away from the sun.
I know, I can't forget this feeling
That keeps me going on.

I know, she knows,
When she looks into my eyes
She understands me,
She feels sorry for me,
They know, I loved him before
He ever saw her face.
But she reached out her hand
To touch his heart.
I love every way about him
I watch him now and understand
" She is more like him"

CAN IT BE

Isn't it love to feel you need
To now you're missing someone
Can't think of all those lonely nights
Without a tear falling.

Is it not love wanting to live my life with you
Living through the good and the bad
Having children together
You and me and then just as one.

Why do I say my love for you is true
Will I know when it's real
Can anyone explain why I feel this way
Is this real or my imagination
Why should I want to find out the truth
Am I afraid of an unfair answer

Can you understand?
I'm not going to hide anymore
I want to live with you
Love you and need you
Us together forever, maybe.

A FACE OF FRIGHT AND ANGER.

Can I blame it on my first lover
All my sadness
Can I blame it on another
All the fright in me
Can I blame it on the future
How my past had been
Can I blame it on the way I find
How spoiled I am inside.

I want to forget that I cannot trust
I want to forget that I cannot love
I want to forget that I cannot be a wife
I want to forget that I cannot need
I want to forget that I cannot hope anymore
I want to forget that I cannot give
I want to forget that I cannot understand

Why! I don't want to be unhappy
Why! I don't want to be afraid
Why! I hate men
Why! I love them
Why! I do
Why! I don't
Why! I
I why
Is this the end of me

GO AWAY.

He didn't say he loved me

He didn't say he cared

He dusted the romantic away

He didn't promise to prove it

He didn't tell a lie

He did keep his dusty pearl away.

HOW DOES A MAN

How does a man think about

His woman

Is she his best friend

Then marriage might be without an end

Do you take good care of your woman

Don't tell her everything

Straight away from your life

For what is a man

Who does not surprise her anymore

When true love can be everlasting

And you would be so naked to her

If she new everything there is to know

So be yourself and take your time to get to know her.

I KNOW.

I know I've been crazy lately

But it's over now.

I know I've been naive lately

But its finished now.

You made me find happiness

You made me want to love again

You make me feel, like you,

Have been the only man in my life.

Haven't been so shy

For a long time now.

Haven't been so glad, inside,

For any man before.

Haven't wished to belong to anyone

For the rest of my life.

But you came and stole my heart

When I was on guard.

IN SORROW.

I hoped my love was a failure
Was preparing for another
When I found that my love
Still loves and grows in another way

In sorrow it began
In sorrow it grew
In sorrow it changed
In sorrow it hid
In sorrow it lived
In sorrow till I die
For in sorrow I found out why

At work, school, enough to do
Only to keep me from you
I'm not worthy for you no more
Now I see I would have been much happier
Just to live a difficult life with you
I'm sad, and my life is much easier

You are difficult to be around
Many things would have changed
I would rather have them now
Cause my love still grows stronger every day.

TO BE FOUND.

I feel alive

Dance the pain away.

I feel the sign

Dance the pain away.

Love is everywhere

I only want you.

So find me and prove it to me

You are worthy for me.

To be walking with me

On the beach.

Just you and me.

So free to love you.

Love you is to

Throw away the past.

Just happy today

So find me.

CLOSE TO ME.

You told me first so shy
Then you told me again
How much I was to you.

I don't have to smile inside me now
You've what I've been looking for
Now I have found you.

I have been thinking so secretly of you
So strongly and now I feel you
Close to me.

I've been holding you
Kissing you too
But just inside of me
Through you are gone from today
I can still feel your lips to mine
This love cannot leave me now.

LOVE IS.

Love is strange and powerful
Full of strength and I suppose
You're one of those people
That hasn't picked that power.

Love is somewhere around you
But does someone show you
Relatives they take you
As one another
But do they love you.

Do you my love, love me
Do you my life, live with me
Do you my heart, hear me.

When I call your name inside me
When I think of you and try
To convince me that I'm yours.

A LOVE SONG

Cause I know, cause I know
That I love you so
Cause I know, cause I know
I would never let you go

I don't want anybody to touch me
They even can't talk to me
I know I am like an ice brake
All closed up inside.

Cause I can't forget the times we had together
How we used to love one another
How we walked in the snow staring up to the sky
Picking out a lucky star.

Nobody could ever have the same effect on me
Like the feelings that went through me
When you reach out to get my hand
I couldn't understand what was happening to me

I try to fight this feeling but it controle´s me
When I look into your eyes I feel happy
You have something special in your blood
Quality no one can measure

I feel better to have written this down,
I can´t think of it will stay there,
I want to show the world in a song,
That my love was so wrong

THE STONE

Our stone is waiting for us
To come and talk around him
About us and our love

We kiss and the sound of
The wind and the waves
Fill our hearts with peace

We walk in the sand
With the northern lights above
And the night is getting dimmer

In our hearts that stone is ours
And misses our warmth
And waits for us alone.

POOR GIRL

I am a poor girl
My life's been bad
Many men have loved me
I still don't understand
What they saw in me
Found in me
But still I am

We would like to listen
To the truth in our souls
But there is always something else
Who tunes up and we have to listen to that!

I would like to see
The stars in the sky
Who reflect in my mind
They are so bright
That I close my eyes

I would like to hear
Words sung by many voices
Who make my house tremble
And shiver so I know how
Small and week one is.

THE LOOKS OF A MAN

How sexy can a man be

I think of when the women scream

I get a chill

I just hope I won't have to

Fight a man like him

For I could be lost

With a scar on my soul

I rather stay at home alone.

HAPPY LIFE.

You brighten up My life

My soul

My will

My skill

My love

My hope

I hope to have a happy life with you.

TO MY DREAM.

I want to see you,

I want to feel you,

I want to know you,

I want to care for you,

But that is too good to be true.

THE TOUCH

When I touch your hair

When I gaze into your eyes

Feel life flying

Feel like I am proud

Having you in my life

Makes me worthy

For another day.

CUTE

Young boy eyes smiled

Felt so touched inside

Wanted to cry but why

He might be my friend

He might understand

Could I ask for more

TO LIKE.

I like to kiss away your tears

Take away your fear

Let you understand.

That the only thing I want

Only thing I need

Is a place in your heart.

TO LOVE IS TO FORGET

I long to sing with you

I long to be with you

And cherish the moments

We will have every day

YOU AND ME

I long to hold you in my arms

And kiss you good night

I hope the love will last

I will not think of the past of you or me

THOUGHTS AND FEELINGS.

I will always love you

Though you never know

Not until I'm gone.

You're personality confuses me

Also how you live and feel

You have not sensed me.

I feel shy when you look at me

Like the sky will fall over me

Who will she be, unknown or me

If you will go

I'll keep your picture

In my mind.

SUPER SKY.

Super sky, super guy,

He is my superior

He is on a mansion

He is in a feeling

He is in a world I like.

I feel him in my mind

Comes to me in the night

Long conversations

Who I cannot remember

Just he was there

My super guy

My freedom

A moment in the sky.

When will I tell him

That he is more than a dream

His eyes with sight

Saved by Jesus

His words about him

Saved my life.

TO DANCE.

I wish I were blond blue eyed

Pale, thin and beautiful,

But would I feel any better

Would you notice me more

I felt great when we danced

All memories disappeared

I watched you but

Did you notice me

You can't imagine how I felt

Not being able to reach to you

Wondering if you were

Laughing in your mind.

I loved you and I still do

I don't think of you

The way I used to do

Will I ever forget

LOVERS.

Their love is like a garden,
Full of flowers,
In all their colors sizes and sorts.

I'm a listener and I acted as,
If I didn't hear but,
I remember hearing them say.

She: You think too much
You never talk
You walk beside me
Like a ghost!

He: I love you more today
Than yesterday but
Less today then
I will tomorrow. (HH)

In everyday life they live within
The clouds, grass, God and
Each other, forever.

They felt a big surprise
Love who lived inside
Was growing so fast.

BLUE NIGHT.

Seems a long time
But still I see
The shadow in
The blue night.

Surprised when I saw
Twins in the moonlight
Playing with their shadows.

Time stopped in my mind
I felt something deep inside
Beating its way to be free.

Two bluebirds came along
They changed tunes in the song
I can feel more love and joy
For now they are four
Dancing in the blue night.

Seems a long time
But still I see
The shadow in
The blue night.

BOY INSIDE MY MAN.

The boy came and rushed to me
He was beautiful strong as a tree
He had a funny look in his eyes.

We were making love
The whole night through
He was a man to me.

He wanted me the way I loved
I loved him to be a part of me
He had everything in this world
Since I got to know his dream of me.

We were dancing in the shade of night
Among the trees'
We watched our kids in the light
They were a growing, a you and I.

We lived in peace and harmony
By the sea
We believed our love would be
Strong and free.

I WILL EVERY DAY.

I will love you forever

We will walk together

Road we were supposed to go.

Sometimes I feel like it's all planned

Like every color in a mind puzzle

Colors who you cannot find in the world

Colors who are different from soul to soul.

Darling when I look at you

I feel like I have never been in love before

Darling when I look into your eyes

I feel like I have never been myself before.

You make me feel like

You have a best friend

You make me feel I'm worthy

You make me think of you all day

You make me wonder about myself

TO PLACE THEIR LOVE.

I placed the candles
were you placed the roses
I lighted them slowly
and you moved to me.

I feel a certain feeling
feeling I never knew,
I live in a certain space,
space I only dreamed of ,
I think of you, then I feel power,
getting loose in my soul,
curling up my back.

I dream of you and then
I feel the tears of joy
coming to my eyes
wanting to cry out loud.

I only want you to kiss me
I like the way we kiss
makes me feel like I've never
kissed anyone but you.

MY LOVE FOR YOU.

My love for you is,

I don't need to hold your hand,

I need to get another look,

Into your eyes',

Then I see what,

Heaven gave to me.

My love for you,

Is growing so peacefully,

Inside of me,

Let me look once more,

Into your eyes',

I love you more,

Than you will ever realize.

TO THINK OF YOU.

I like to think of you

And give you

A poem I made for you

And I sing it to you.

The gift I gave you

Was not much but

It's all that I owned

In this world.

It was a poem to you

and I know you liked it more ,

Than anything else from me.

You see I love you,

Dont want to,

Turn my back on you

In my mind

They way I saw you

In my dream.

My dream of you

Every time something evil gets to me

I try to think of you

Every time my patience breaks down

I try to see your face in my mind

Every time my soul is filled with anger

I try to dream of you.

Every time everyday I need to hear your voice

I'm so deeply in love with you

Every time everyday I need to see you face

I need you like the air that I breathe

Every time I look into you're eyes

Everytime I look into your soul,

I see how wrong I was.

Every time I try to make it up to you

The fool in me that left you

Every time I hope for a future for us

I can't think of one without you.

Everytime I need something

You know I need you and your love.

TO STEVE

You were in my dream

Your green eyes were watching me

How long will it be

until we will it be

together like in my dream.

If there is a future for me

leave me a place in your heart

If there is someone out there

for you then let her be me.

Your strong body

I felt you in my dream

You were shy to me

then I set you free.

Who is out there

is it you, who I see

Will we meet

I'll be ready for thee.

THE AMERICAN CAT

He was in my dream tonight

He had a hold on me close to me , close to me

He was my long lost friend

Since I was a child come to me, come to me

He was like the boy who had

No eyes to see but he cried for me, cried for me

Like a cat in the night

He came to me , came to me

He stared at me with his green eyes

He was watching me, asking me

I share my thought of him with someone else

He had a face I had sought who might

Keep me in love, I feel so weak

His body was so close to me, close to me

He was everything to me, the lights went out

I stood alone with my memory, memory, I feel his heartbeat

Heartbeat in my soul, he stared at me with

His green eyes like a cat in the night.

TO LIKE LOVE

I look into your eyes

I hold you in my arms

Love can be a sacrifice

To bend without breaking

Sometimes I feel I need you

Sometimes I like to tell you my secrets.

TO ME

Do you want to love me tonight

I want you to hold me always

Do you need to be loved by me

I want you to love me always

Do you think I can make you

The happiest man in the world

Do you know that I am the

Happiest woman for you.

THE LIES OF LOVE

It all begun few months ago
It started quickly and
Finished wisely

I thought I was loved
Really cared for
And gave my love in return

You don't give all your love
To someone you
Don't know very well

When you get no love back
Only pretty words
Who could mean a lot

You told me so many words
Without a feeling for them
How could you have meant them

You wonder why
You where such a fool
To believe such a heart.

THIS SONG.

This song I sing to you
Is a so long it's true
Try to feel the way I do, try to
Understand why I'm going away.

I can't forget memories
What happened to me
Why can't I do what I want
Why can't I go where I long to be.

I believe in good things
I live in bad ways
I seem to forget golden rules
I seem to remember them always.

TOO LONELY TO LEARN.

I know you are never
going to be mine
I know you are never
going to share your time.

I can feel it
I can see it
your love belongs
to someone else.

You have decided to
give all your love
to that someone else.

Please say you have
chanced your mind
about me.

I need you,
And your love,
don't make me lonely.

TWO FEET AGAIN.

I was in love with a man last year
The most wonderful time in my life.
I was blind by the words he said
To me in the heat of the night.

Now I think what went wrong
Why did I tell him to go
For I knew I loved him so
And didn't want him to know.

I lay and wonder what will change
My bitterness to fun.
I cry for the love I have lost
For now I know I was wrong.

I should have asked for his forgiveness,
And lived with him my life.
Really hoping he would learn to love me
As I really am.

I thought his words were all lies
My pride was hurt.
Thought he didn't take me as an equal
I could have stayed and learned how to love.

And learned to walk on my two feet again.
And stand by whom I am.

WHERE IS TRUE LOVE

Here am I waiting for a call

Wanting to hear your voice

Whispering words into my ear

Words a girl never forgets

I know our love will live tomorrow

I hope I can give you more of myself

I feel shy and will try to go away

If you wouldn't stand up to the things you say

I love you so much I don't think

Of an end to my love

I need you so much that I will not go away

For I don't want to live in this world without you.

DREAMING.

Dreams have to end
Not going to spend
My time just dreaming

Don't want to pretend
That I've forgotten you
When I am dreaming.

Need to cry out loud
But huss I can only cry
When I am dreaming.

Lonely As ever
Without nobody knowing
That's why I am dreaming.

If you have a dream and
If our dreams should meet
There will be two of us dreaming.

If you would see
The light in me
The love for thee
You would be dreaming.

ONLY A WOMAN WITH YOU.

I wonder what I could be
I wonder if I am here for thee
If I can love you and be free
Makes me want to be just me.

Then why should my sexuality
Confuse me and make me lonelier
I guess I am not a woman
Unless you are here with me.

I would want to have both
You my love and my freedom
To be as I am and not to be
Hiding myself away from thee.

I wonder if you are like me
Willing to share love
And your life with me
Because I am lonely.

When I think or dream of you
I feel I am in love with you
I feel I am only a woman if I have
Hope of sharing you and to love you.

I WONDER IF

Sooner that later
I will meet you.
I will try to
Avoid to.

For you might
Have the code.
That has the access
To my heart.

After that there would be,
no looking back,
I would be completely,
In love with you.

Would I have to
Worry about if .
You're feelings for me
Would change easily.

And I would have
No way to go back.
To what I was before
Or where I came from.

SILLY YOUNG

When I was younger

I hoped I could fall in love

Surprised to be

Like a flower tree

You came to me

Fell on your knee

I like you to stay with me

Like you were family

You said please too me

Let me stay with thee

And with your Christmas tree.

LITTLE INDIAN BOY.

I can never forget
Those brown eyes
I can never forget
His brown hair.
I dream of him sometimes
Always smiling
I speak to him somewhere
And tell him what.
I never told him when
He was still mine.
I love you
I miss you
I smile for you
My little hero.

I will never forget that smile
I can never forget his eyes.

I sometimes cry for what I have lost
I sometimes hear you comfort me
So I tell him what I should have
Told him when he was still alive.

I love you
I miss you
I smile to you
I'm your hero
I will keep on

WHY ME, IMAGINE ITS ME.

How can you forgive me
How can you please me
There's more love in you
Then I ever hoped tell be.

Why did I leave you lonely
Ashamed in the night
Knowing I loved you
But not strong enough
To be beside you.

Now there is a hope in me
That my lord will forgive me
If not I don't blame him
For I'm a fool, he knows.

You are different from others,
Why is this man
Coming into my dream
What does he want from me

I'm tempted to be in love
How can someone
Fall in love in a dream,
Don't ask me how

LOST LOVE.

I feel like I have lost you

A long time ago

But don't you worry

They way I am can't

Easily be changed by you.

So don't you loose your love

For someone who is not true

I am hoping it will make me

Better somehow for someone

Else than you.

I think about how clean

Ones love can be

For someone who

Feels only sixteen

I should have left you a long time ago.

SO WHY.

You know I'm leaving
You don 't want me to
So you give me things
To try to make me stay
But can't you in another way
Tell me , you want me to stay
I don't know what to do
Can anyone give me a clue
I need a little push off my throne
I don 't want to leave you alone.
My soul says
You ' re so young, learn a lot more,
Live it through say goodbye.
Then I told myself,
Come out to the land
Let's walk in the nature
Let's enjoy prettiness of light
I heard someone say,
You miss me I know
You will be lonely, believe me.
Kept on saying,
It's difficult to have someone,
Who loves you more than himsclf
Don 't you know
It's hard to leave.
I got to make up my mind,
And I said,
I'm not worthy for your love
Find someone like you
For I only think of myself.

TO KNOW YOU

Now I know a little bit more
Now I want a little bit of you
Now I want to get to know you more

You don't have to give me things
But I like your way of thinking
Of giving to me.

You don't have to give me things
Only to please me but you I can have
Almost anytime I want you.

Today I look at you
Then I look at me
And will it always be
When I look at me
I remind me of you.

WHY ME.

Hold me tight
like a leaf
hold me all night
For I will heal.

Come my love
Lets enjoy songs
Of love and peace.

Lets sing together
the song who doesn't
have to end.

Talk to me about yourself
and you're love for me
enjoy me while I'm here.

I love your big brown eyes
also your black hair
why do you love me.

A FLOWER WHO NO ONE WANTS TO HURT.

I look forward to see you
I know something good brought
Us together
It won't be so easily broken apart
I'm not a wise woman
But he makes me feel like a flower
Who no one wants to hurt.

I feel fear in my heart
Maybe he would change his mind
I know in my heart
I'm just afraid of me.

I trust him
I love him
I need him
I want him

Is he the only man I could trust
Is he the only man I could love
I don't want him to know
And stay with him
For the rest of my life.

LEARNS TO.

I need you like you need me

A love so rarely found

Has come our way.

I'm a Cinderella girl

Raised on the streets

Abused by people who use

Others innocence and kindness.

I learned not to trust

But still I do, only you.

I learned to cheat

But still i dont ,i couldn´t cheat on you

I learned to be cruel

But i cant be cruel to you

And no soul is cruel

Only learns how to .

I DO.

Why do I look so peaceful

At the mirror.

Why do I smile

In my sleep.

Why do I need you

More every day.

I think I'm in love with you

But can I be sure

You can't believe I'm yours

Can't you see!

The spark in my eyes.

You can't believe I'm yours

For there is no girl like me

Who's willing and caring

For you each day.

A LONG TIME AGO

Once I had an old memory
Who was reborn in my mind
Now an old feelings had been duged up
From the grave I had closed long time ago.

Once I knew love and was afraid
Now I can love without a fear
Sometimes you dream about things
Who don't matter anything to anyone else.

An older man was in my mind
I felt closer to him than anyone else
I was in love with a much older man
I like his character that was gentle and sweet

Could you imagine me with an older man
I needed him then, like I thought I always would
Some birds learn to listen to their own hearts
And stay as themselves, though they knew others

This bird felt so free to be herself
This bird felt so in love and thought she's mad
Somehow I like the feeling that filled my heart
With joy to feel you need, makes you wonder could I leave.

TOURIST

A lost tourist traveling in Greece

Lost in the land and here I am

Walking on a dusty country road

With memories in my mind.

Sleeping on the beach

Woke up in the heat

Finding him gone

If I hadn't been so blind

I want to see his face again

I'm on a country road

Where does it end?

He's so much like the man I want

I hear a wagon getting near

I would know that smile anywhere

His dark eyes' that black hair

Shining in the sunlight.

HOPING STOP

Don't tell me to stop

Loving you

Don't tell me to stop

Then I'll give you a hoping stop

Don't you show me that

You're though

I'll hit you hard

On your hip

You give me a spin baby

Don't you go to sleep oh no

How could you

When I am doing it to you

I am not through yet

Come on hold me tight

For the rest of the night

For a hoping stop

A hopins stop.

WAS LOVE REAL

Is it not great to have
A love like ours
Is it not great to have
Accomplished you

I love to hear your
Lonely voice
I love to tell you
How great you are

You told me that
I am unforgettable
You told me that
I was your only love

Let's make love tonight
So I can stand
The fight another day
Reality is cruel sometimes

Sleep tight in my arms
Keep me here
At least this time.

EVER SINCE YOU WENT AWAY.

I'm feeling helpless, with a headache

My stomach so full, slept too much.

Studied too little, didn't work

Haven't talked to anyone for a long time.

Turned on the TV, didn't want to think

Afraid of the feeling that wanted me to write

Simple thoughts and feelings

Who no one wants to read

Am I the only one to understand

This is my destiny.

I deceived myself, swept that thought away

Here crept another sinner, we are all the same

Went into my shell, what is wrong or right

We just do what they all do.

Say later we will all realize

To listen to our hearts

Then we won't be this way.

TRUSTING YOU.

Can it be, that you're going away
Can it be, you're walking out
Can it be, that you're leaving me behind.
Can it be, I wonder why
My crying face all alone
And you're walking out the door
I say can it be, can it be.
I am amazed and my crying eyes
I always seemed so happy on the outside
Our house no longer a home
For you never wanted to find out
Can it be, can it be?
I see you're face clearly in my mind
I am amazed what it might be telling me
Can it be, can it be
You're crying eyes are thinking of me.

No longer do I doubt
No longer do I think
That you will leave me
Or be bad to me
For I know you love me
For I feel now the way
You are thinking of me.

HAPPY BIRTHDAY.

I often feel bad to know the fact
And it's hard to say
He knows something's about me
When I was only trying to play.

I would not want you to stop
Telling me those nice things
About your great Heart
And how lovers love can be.

Why does my heart refuse
To know the truth about him
Encourage me please, I think
I can't live without him.

IT'S USELESS.

It's useless, can't help it

This grows from day to day

When I'm hoping it will fade away.

Will she take you away

Kiss you when I can see

I would go, never come back,

You saw me, I know

I tried not to let show

Watched you when

You didn't notice,

It's me you need, I need you

Time goes so fast, I feel so sad

Talking to you, well you didn't hear.

Why did I have to be so shy

Can't talk to you

Without trembling inside.

It does not matter what you'll do

What you will feel,

Were you'll be,

I think I will always love you.

IN LOVE-IN SORROW.

In love in sorrow

He could never love me

He could never get to know me

I hid to well

How could I know

Maybe he couldn't have loved me

I never get to know.

Am I going to be stupid again

I could let him know, or wait.

No, he couldn't love me,

Would he look at me

I could go into hiding again.

And never show my soul.

To anyone else.

THE LOST AFFECTION

He could never be hers

She wanted one man in her life

Now she looks at another boy

Who is like him

He belongs to another woman

So much time has passed

He doesn't get out of her mind

She looks into the eyes of her husband

He doesn't know

What she is thinking now

Can it be

Oh God why did this happen

I didn't want anyone else

Now she wants everything else

For the most precious thing

In her life and soul is missing

missing

Forever apart in her life.

Nothing can change that

She thinks and she hopes

Only when I die, then.

HIS SURPRISE

You don't know how lucky you are

Sharing love and life with him

You can be happy from now on

For you are proud of him and his love

You share time with him

Who many others would like to share

You are the best for him

Be proud of yourself

I feel like you are happy

And I am happy to tell you

That you are his presence

His equal friend

BIG TALK

Who am I

To sit here

Calling you my friend

When you are spending time

With someone else.

Who are you

Why do I want

To spend my time with you

When I know

That you love

That someone else so true,

If love would have been

The only thing in life

I would have died

I am still alive and preparing for

Another birth of love.

BECAUSE OF ME

I know someone's unhappy
He's lonely and cries a lot
But what can I do
Is it because of me
That he is feeling blue.
I'm sorry for I don't love you
I'm sorry for I don 't need any man
I'm sorry for I don't understand you
Let your wound heal
Leave me now
I don 't want to be cruel
Forget me now
I know I can never
Live like you
I want to be free
I don 't need a baby
To feel like a hole woman
I don't need a family
That' s depends on me
Or a luxury
All I need is myself
Peace and harmony
I'm not a dream
Nor a fantasy
I'm real and believe me
I can feel

So stay away from me
Please, please, don't hurt me.

GOODBYE TO YOU.

People surprised that
I don't want you no more
They didn't have to live
With you and care for you at all.

I am not the kind of a woman
That loves a man that much
That she would give him her soul
For she is also a feeling personality.

Don't you know I can't ever stop being myself
I am going to be myself
For evermore so you have to
Face up to that.

That I don't love you
The way I used to do
I don't want to hold you
Feel sick to -look at you.

When you are feeling pity for yourself
Because your mother who died many years ago
Crying on my pillow now
To make me want you for sympathy.

You always think of yourself
Pity because your children
Are in a safe place with
Their mother oh no.

CONSEQUENCES OF A KISS.

A midnight hint to give away
Love to a man I thought
Would understand.

If he is man enough
To care for me.
Then he must be smart enough
To keep me.

He deceived me with
Nice words and his face
Wasn't enough to hold me.

The consequences of a kiss
Was growing inside of me.

Today I don't regret
When I look at my son's face
Whom I love so much

He loves me
He is my biggest love
For uncondisonely
He is my best mistake.

THAT YEAR.

I thought I had been loved
By him that year.
I thought I had been in
Wonderland with him again
I thought it was called romance
I wanted to be loved by him
I hoped my love wouldn't die for him
Now I see it was wrong
I feel his love is gone
His love had gone away.

I thought I couldn't do without him
I hoped something would change
I wanted him never to let me go
I really thought he loved me so
I was a fool, so cruel,
For he walked out on me
Lonely and empty inside
I carry on I know
So fare well, forgive me now
You don't walk out on your children
You don't walk out on your love.

FEELINGS FOR YOU.

You make me feel like a woman
You're the only man I want
Our child will be our affection
I look forward of having one.

You don't know that I know
That I carry our child
You wouldn't suspect it now
Not unless I would let you know.

Time goes so fast
I don't want to be lied to
I want to do things when
I want to and choose when too.

You said goodbye to me
And I was with child
Was it all in my mind
I misunderstood your feelings for me.

IT IS RIGHT.

I'm in love
It feels good
He loves me
in a different way.

When I'm asleep I hear him say
I love you so much
I don't know why
See you soon
I cry in my dreams.

I don't want to believe you
That's it's the way it's going to be
And I ask
Will you always love me
Can I trust you
Do I have to stay

Search for tomorrow
Don't think of yesterday
Do I want to stay
Don't make me cry again
I'm sorry if I go away
But I come running back
Missing you is very hard
Maybe I'll never go again.

LOVE SEEMS YOUNG.

In a song, love seems young

In my mind there was no one

In a lifetime you couldn't know

In one's life things don't go slow.

Simple life and a clean mind

I pray for thee

Song lives on and changes

So I feel a tear falling down.

How can you realize the change in me

When you hardly knew me before

You could come and laugh with me

Were we could feel the force in me.

In nature there is a certain force

Strong and beautiful

It can change the weather and

Make mountains fall.

WITHOUT WORDS

Once I saw a lady

All dressed in white

Walking on the shore

Looking at the northern lights

She had been so alone

For such a long time

That she forgotten how

It was like to love

A man came walking

Towards her wearing blue

Looked at her eyes , then

She reached our for his hand

They started walking

And every day they meet

Walking this lonely shore together

Their love does not need any words.

TO ME BEFORE YOU

No man has reached my soul

No man talks to me

Like you do

You are special

No one is like you

I am in love

I know I can make you happy

We were meant to be

To love and to care for

Were we meant to live together.

THE FILM.

I saw a film tonight
I was thrilled
Felt so glad inside
I felt so much happiness
I felt so many feelings
Like the feelings I felt for you
I needed to talk
I wanted to be listened to
But look I have no friend
Who wants to hear

I'm so glad I want to cry
I'm so glad I want to die
I'm so in love
I'm so lonely inside

Now I see it's only me
Who I can wonder about myself
Now I know it's only me
Who can understand.

I see myself alone
You really didn't 't come
I only got myself to count on

IT HURTS TO LOVE YOU

Feel the sun

Smell the air

Taste the rain.

Think of you

Waiting over here

For you and why.

Never fall in love again

It hurts too much

So I will try to stop dreaming of you.

I will try to let go of you

My dear if you think that

You were not meant for me

Let me know and I will let go of thee.

WHAT I FOUND.

I found that my heart had been
Closed for a long time.
I found that I had feelings
Laughter and affection inside.

To put that in a box in your heart
And just close that down.
Hide it away from the world
And from who you and me.

Will I ever find anyone that
Deserved to be trusted by me
I can then stop being in a box
Away from reality and cruelty.

Would I deserve such a man
Will I find him
Do you think I can
Whatever you may say
I'll find him my own way.

Then I could open up a box from my heart
And forget I'm real
I would only feel
Forget everything and everyone else
And surrender my love to you.

COME ON.

Come on baby, let's sing a song
Come on baby, let's flirt around
Were here some kids, just having fun
Come on baby, show me you're the one.

I am here, I am free,
waiting for a you and me
somewhere I am to be
you're lover for eternity.

I am no one night stand
for you will see that I am
so shy that it's useless
To fall in love with me.

Just a hint for you,
That i don´t come in two,
I am just what you see,
For you are mine to be.

So singing to you i say,
Lets just have fun today,
It´s amazing what you can do,
When you get into my mind , would you?

So stay back, for I don't want
To fall in love with you
you would be stuck with me
just from now on to eternity.

WITHOUT A PRIZE.

Can't buy my love
Can't buy your love
That is just ridicules.

You can't fake a feeling
In a dream
There is no one to take
That away from me.

You wonder what it means,
You can´t rest easy,
When you don´t dream,
for dreams don´t die on you.

It is you who dies on your dreams
It is only you,
They're for you, to stick to you
For dreams don't die on you.

So I keep on dreaming
My dreams are just for3 me,
And only for me to see,
So sweet dreams to me.

STOCKHOLM SYNDROME.

To be in love you think
Rather for sympathy
Than it actually because
Of his personality.

It's always him so hurt
For this or that
Bad excuses for
Hurting you so much.

Only he can take
The burden of how he feels
Only he can fake
These lying tears.

Knowing him inside out
Always in fear
Anxiety attack daily
To look at him near.

Still lying to herself
Convincing herself
It's all in her mind
He can't be that
Therefore it's either
Divorce or death.

ILLUSIONS.

What am I doing to you

What am I doing to myself

It is not a mystery no more

I'll never love again, never again.

He is the only one I can love

The only one who understands

The only one who would love me

For who I am.

Who am I to say

That he thinks that way

Is it right am i abusing you ?

Trying to hide, lieing all the time

CONFUSION.

You would like to hold me
You would like to touch me
But you aren't going to.

You would like to kiss me
You would like to love me
I'm not going to let you.

I'm going to let you know
While we are here
That I'm not your kind.

I'm trying to live a nice life
I'm not looking for a husband
It might take me one night to realize
It could take me thousand years.

That I want to be noticed
Loved and cared for
And be your friend
Are you that man

I like to have a friend
I like to belong to him
But will he realize
What I need from him

THE THOUGHT OF YOU.

The thought of you
Makes me feel
Happy and true.

The thought of you
Makes me feel
So strong for you

It makes me wonder
If there is someone like me
Out there who is true to oneself

To live by oneself
And to agree only too
What I can accept from myself

I have to live with the thought
That I don't want to do you wrong
For I couldn't face that in the mirror
That I failed you in some way.

If you are thinking like me
You don't want to hurt me
For no one deserves that behavior
Then you are learning about yourself.

We are all the same inside
A soul, a body
A spirit, a DNA
Who cares, maybe I do.

YOU.

Have you ever been in love
Do you know what to need is
To be sure what love is
Can you ever forgive
I thought I was in love
I was still in pain.

You are a friend,
You ask me about myself
Honestly I cannot lie to you
I need to tell the truth
You know me to well.

My heart belongs to him
I can never forget him
But he didn't want me
He couldn't love me.

I played a game
Wasn't myself
That's why he never
Got to know me.

Made a fool of myself
By fooling others
Made a fool of them
Who tried to believe me

WHAT TO FIND.

All I needed from you
Was honesty
All I wanted was respect.

You didn't have to offer me
Anything except,
A place in your heart.

A place in your heart
All I needed was a smile
A look, a touch.

You brushed me off
With treating me bad
And making it clear.

That you could never
Grow up and learn how to
Treat the one that loves you.

The one you say you love
With a little dignity
Honesty and believe me that's love.

A WOMAN TO YOU.

If I was a woman to you

And if you would never see

Anything else in me

Then you're feelings for me

Wouldn't be

Like the feelings I feel for you.

For I see so many colors in your soul

I like you in so many ways

You could be my best friend

You are a person

I've been seeking for

I've need nothing more

I am a woman

Who wants you

BUTTERFLY.

You might look at me
I might look at you
Somehow I feel you near
So I start to fear
That wishful thinking
Is taking me there
I am already trying
To take care.

If you might wonder
Were we have been
Then I keep on dreaming
So I can find you there
Come on my dear
Try to understand
For with you I am a woman
Who flies away with you.

Might be a human butterfly
You make me want to be
Just here for thee
I know that's silly
But I really feel like
You might be wondering
About me and I dream
How would it really be
If you were here with me.

TO BE NEAR YOU.

When I look at you
I feel like your face
Is a very special one
I love to touch you.

When I touch you
I feel like your body
Is a special one
I love to hold you.

When I hold you,
I feel like your eyes,
Are looking at my soul,
I love to be with you.

When I am with you
I feel like your love
Is the best thing that
Happened to me.

I love to be near you,
Today, tonight,
I tell you.

THE HIDDEN LOVE

Do you know
How much
I love you

I want to
Hold you in
The night

Then we will
Sail away
On the wave
Of love

Don't you know
My life is devoted
To you and that
Love can be forever

You see I need you
But you stay away
I might never know you
Cause later could be too far away.

SOMEHOW I WAIT.

Somehow I wait for
Snow to fall
Somehow I long for
A touch of sunshine.

Somehow I stay till
The morning comes
Somehow I cry for
That eternity will come.

Somehow I laugh at
All the tears I've cried
Somehow I wish to,
Hold you in my arms.

Somehow is now,
So lets play.
Somehow is more.
Face it I would stay.

Somehow I play
Ask me to stay
For that day.

I WISH FOR.

Today I wish for
A happy day with you
Today I wish for
A nice evening too
Today I wish for
Long night with you.
Today I wish for
A life with you
Today I wish for
A nice tomorrow too.

I hope you wish too
That you and I are true
Future behold I'm looking
Out for you.

Tomorrow I wish for
I will meet you soon
Tomorrow I wish for
That you would be true
Tomorrow I wish for
A me and a you
So good night and
Dream two
I think I love you
So beware of me
Have I even seen you
Where are you
I know I haven't met you
Could you love me
Honest, try to.

WHERE LOVE LIVES

You might wonder
If it is not better
For me to be here

I might wonder
If it is not better
For me to be there

But honey you know that
No matter where we would be

Home is where love is
Home is where love is

So I say in my heart
I hope we get a start
To be friends and etcetera

For time is the most
Precious thing to me
You know how I feel for thee

So I keep on hoping
For time ahead
Could you love me

Home is where love is
Home is where love is.

LOVE FOR YOU.

Love for you
Is somewhere inside of me
Crying out for
A gentle touch.

Love for you
Is somewhere hiding
Its tears away
From this world.

Love for you
Is somewhere growing
In my soul and in my blood
I wait for you

My love for you
Is quietly growing
Inside of me for a
Day with you
Is all and more

A memory too
I hide my face
Away from you
I need you too
Like I long for
A night or day
Until eternity
Will take me away.

THE TENDER TUNE

I wish upon a star

That you would forgive me

I know I did bad

By leaving

I did no good

By staying

For I love another

I cant live in a lie anymore

II

I wish my life

With you would be

Like a happy dream

I wish my love to be

Happy with me

I sometimes wish

I wouldn't want you

But I do

Wish I could go

And be with you

III

In that time I think

I will tremble

Like a tune in a

Tender song

Time will pass

Like the tears

That I cry

I keep on

Wondering why

I feel so much for you.

MY MAN AND ME.

My man to be is no sex symbol
My man to be is no sugar pop
My man to be is no brown-eyed gigolo
My man is not

He is a man, he loves me,
For who I am,
He is a man, I love him,
For who he is.

I'm not a pretty woman
I'm not sexy at all
I'm not a pretty body
I'm not.

When we would be together
Everything is out somewhere
Then we would talk over things
Who we want to discuss
Then I realize more
How much part
He has in me.

Would we share many ideas
Is he always active
Would he allow me to do
What I like
So now I'm photographing
And writing songs.

DADDY'S GIRL

There I am is my mind
dancing for daddy of mine
I'm a daddy's girl

He helps me every day
He feeds me and dresses me
cleans up my mess
for he is my dad

I can't think of a life
without him
He's always there for me
even in hard times.

I sing and dance for him
and we laugh
we have a good life
Shall I sing for you.

What do you want to do
What do you want to say
When daddy's off to work
Haha I go to mommy then

THE SIGN

Alone I am, In a dream

dead dog serius

listening to a lullaby

Alone I am

in a dream

dead dog silent

listening to a lullaby

a lullaby about

a unicorn and

a beast.

and a child thanked me

I was not alone anymore

in my day dream.

good pillow talk

The child said

and I hear Gods voice

saying thank you

in a modest way

should I write it down I ask

" we should " He said to me.